THE REAL
ESTATE
INVESTOR
SURVIVAL GUIDE

25 MISTAKES YOU CAN'T AFFORD TO MAKE WHEN INVESTING IN REAL ESTATE

BY

JEFF LEIGHTON

Important Disclaimers

Table of Contents

Author's Note 7

Introduction 8

Section 1: Not Moving Fast Enough 11

Section 2: Overcomplicating Things For The Seller 13

Section 3: Listening To The Wrong People 16

Section 4: Biting Off More Than You Can Chew 21

Section 5: Making Offers Without Using
            The MAO Formula.. 25

Section 6: Overdoing The Renovation For The Area 27

Section 7: Underestimating The Repair Costs 30

Section 8: Location, Location, Location 33

Section 9: Be Careful Of Partnerships 36

Section 10: The Market Does Not Always Go Up................ 41

Section 11: Make Sure You Have The Right Contractor
            For The Job 44

Section 12: Avoid This When Listing Your Property 48

Section 13: Run Your Own Numbers.................................... 52

Section 14: Trusting Everyone 55

Section 15: Quitting Your Full-Time Job Too Soon........... 58

Section 16: Falling In Love With A House
Instead Of The Numbers...................................61

Section 17: Not Screening Your Tenants............................ 63

Section 18: Getting To The Next Level As
A Real Estate Investor...................................... 67

Section 19: No Leads = No Deals...71

Section 20: Burning Bridges...74

Section 21: Focus On Getting To Closing............................77

Section 22: Become Friends With The Seller...................... 80

Section 23: Every Neighborhood Is Great........................... 83

Section 24: Protect Your Assets.. 86

Section 25: Becoming Known In The Community 89

Conclusion 92

About The Author... 94

Author's Note

This book contains additional resources that I use on a daily basis as a real estate investor. Since I could not physically include these in the book, they are all available to download for free on my website www.jeff-leighton.com. That includes my deal analyzer, repair estimator, example contracts, marketing pieces that I use, recommended resources, helpful videos, and much more.

Introduction

I remember it as if it was yesterday. I was struggling in the real estate business. Trying to make it as a real estate investor can be tough, especially when you are getting started. It seemed I was making every mistake in the business and although I would have successful deals here and there, I was still making a ton of mistakes.

Maybe you can relate to this and have made some of your own mistakes along the way. When you try to find advice for what mistakes to avoid, you can find an array of information that may or may not be relevant to real estate investing.

In this guide I have collected all the major mistakes that I have made as a real estate investor as well as mistakes that investor friends of mine have made. What I reveal in this guide are straight-to-the-point stories and examples of real-world situations that you will find yourself in as a real estate investor. Not only will I give you examples and stories, but I will also tell you the moral of the story and how to avoid it in the future.

Why should you listen to me? I make six figures per year as a real estate investor and have been mentored by some of the top real estate investors in the world. I'm not saying that to brag but instead to give you an idea of where my advice is coming from.

Real estate investing is one of the most exciting, interesting, and profitable businesses out there, but as in any business there are major pitfalls that you need to avoid. I believe one of the best ways to learn is to learn from mistakes, and ideally not your own mistakes. In this book we go over real-life real estate investing stories that have happened both to myself and some investors friends of mine. We will start with some of the more basic mistakes I've made and work our way up to some of the more advanced mistakes you need to know about if you are to become a savvy real estate investor.

Learning about these stories could save you literally hundreds of thousands of dollars as well as the headache associated with going to court and getting involved in legal action. I would recommend reading this book at least two or three times since it is relatively short and to the point, and at the end of each chapter I leave you with the lesson learned or the moral of the story and what NOT to do. These stories and lessons will make you a better real estate investor if you learn from them.

Not Moving Fast Enough

In real estate investing, good deals do not last long. If you are new to real estate investing and you are doing marketing, you will sometimes stumble on amazing deals. And when you do, you have to jump on them and be all over those leads. I'll tell you a quick story of what I mean. Most professional real estate investors will also tell you that a good off-market deal only last 24-48 hours. Then it's gone to one of your competitors.

When I was first getting started with direct mail marketing, I got a very hot lead on a Sunday. The property was absentee owned, the seller wanted to get rid of it ASAP, and the house needed a ton of work. What I should have done was immediately run numbers, call that guy back, and make him an offer within the hour or even within 30 minutes. Instead, what I did was wait until Monday, thrilled that I had this great lead to follow up with. I even wrote it down as the first item on my to-do list for Monday with excitement.

By the time I called him back on Monday morning, he had already gone with another offer and the deal was gone. These motivated seller types of leads don't happen every day, and I was devastated. I had waited too long and lost out on what would have been a significant six-figure rehab profit.

MORAL OF THE STORY: The moral of the story is that good deals do not last long. If you find a motivated seller, someone who says they want to sell ASAP and the house needs a lot of work, then you need to drop everything and make them an offer. Most leads are not motivated, so keep that in mind. Therefore, when you do come across a hot lead, you have to take action.

Overcomplicating Things For The Seller

With real estate investing you need to make things as simple and straightforward as possible for the seller. If you get a motivated seller lead, keep in mind they often want to get rid of the property as soon as possible in the easiest way possible. The sales price they are looking for is often not their first priority.

One of the best deals I ever got was at the expense of another investor who had tried and blew it big time when working with this particular seller. This investor had tried to set up a complicated partnership with the seller instead of just offering to purchase the property. The seller called me exasperated saying that she wanted to sell ASAP and the house needed a lot of work. In other words, the perfect lead. She told me she had been under contract with another investor who wanted to partner with her on the deal and then split the profit three to six months down the road once the house was renovated.

The only problem was that the other investor was not listening to what the seller wanted and was overcomplicating things. The seller wanted to get rid of the house; she did not want to do any type of formal partnership with someone she didn't know. Instead of just making an "as is" offer with a fast close, the investor decided to offer a partnership. When the seller called me, I ran my number ASAP and gave her an offer with a fast close and in "as is" condition. The seller accepted my offer, and the other investor missed out on a big deal because of overcomplicating things.

MORAL OF THE STORY: The moral of the story is to listen to what the seller is saying and keep things simple and easy for them. "A confused mind says no." Always remember that quote. If you are more of an experienced investor, then by all means it sometimes makes sense to partner with the seller or do some type of seller financing. However, if you are new to real estate investing, I would stick to the bread and butter of making simple "as is" offers with a fast close and no real estate agent commissions. Make things so simple that your grandmother could understand.

Listening To The Wrong People

Real estate investing has more MIS-information than almost any industry out there. Everybody has an opinion on the business and thinks they know what they are talking about. Most of the time their information is coming from the one house they bought 10 years ago and maybe something they heard on the news. You need to only listen to the top 1% of real estate investors, people that are out there buying houses as a business and are successful doing so.

Being in the real estate investing business for so long, I have heard some of the most absurd and far-fetched advice on investing. Here are the three people I have seen most commonly give horribly misguided and sometimes completely made up advice.

The first person would be your local know-it-all real estate agent. Let me start with a disclaimer that many real estate agents are amazing. However, I think we all have that one local real estate agent in our area who seems to be very negative towards investing. They say things like, "You just can't find investment deals," "Flipping doesn't work," "Investing in real estate is a scam," or any number of pieces of misinformation. The problem with agents giving this advice is that they have never invested successfully in real estate themselves and of course they are not full-time real estate investors. I know of one agent in particular who lost money on a flip about 10 years ago and then drastically overpaid on another home. He is still bitter about it and will tell you every reason why real estate flipping, or even investing for that matter, does not work. Stay far away from these people.

Let me give you an analogy with basketball. Let's say you wanted to become a professional star basketball player. You would not get advice from someone who got cut from their middle school basketball team and is still mad about it. You should only get basketball advice from professional basketball or high level players and you should only get real estate investing advice from professional real estate investors.

Keep in mind that the majority is wrong about just about everything. If the person giving you advice is not currently investing in real estate or does not have a track record of investing in real estate, that means they are completely lacking in credibility. I don't care how many theories or master's degrees they have. Run as far away from this negative influence as possible and immerse yourself in real estate investing podcast interviews with successful interviews, books, seminars, and any other successful real estate mentors you can model.

The second source of non-stop sheer nonsense are CNN and Fox News headlines. The mainstream media is a big business. As a business it is their job to attract viewers. One way they do that is by coming up with dramatic and astonishing headlines and by making claims that are often false or completely misrepresented.

They will use cherry-picked statistics to show why house flipping is dead or why house flipping is back.

The truth is, at any point in the economy you could probably manipulate some statistic to make either claim. However, these are not claims made by real estate investing pros. Professional real estate investors buy houses in up and down markets. They understand that although the real estate market is continually changing, there will always be an opportunity for investors because there will always be motivated sellers and opportunities to add value to properties.

Lastly, the people close to you, including friends, family, co-workers, neighbors, or others, will often try to talk you out of real estate investing. They will tell you that it's too competitive, it's a scam, you can't do it anymore, and you should just get a regular steady job like them. Again, these are not the people you should be getting real estate investing advice from. I am shocked on a daily basis by how willing and able people with no successful track record in real estate investing are to give out real estate investing advice as if it's an absolute certainty. Most people just never got the information on how to be a real estate investor and think it's a fantasy, when in reality there are everyday people investing successfully in real estate.

MORAL OF THE STORY: The moral of the story is only to get real estate investing advice from successful real estate entrepreneurs. The ways to find these people is to buy books like this one on Amazon, listen to real estate investing podcasts, and find a real estate investing mentor who can show you the ropes. When I was getting started with real estate investing, I read as many books as possible, listened to podcast interviews of successful investors, and paid for a real estate mentor whose program showed me how to find off-market deals on a consistent basis.

Biting Off More Than You Can Chew

For your first real estate investment deal, whether it's a wholesale or rehab, I would highly recommend starting small and starting local, in your backyard. You don't know how many times I talk to a student who is asking me about some large-scale development they want to do when they haven't even flipped their first house or even got any seller leads yet. Alternatively, they might ask me about virtual wholesaling in some other state when they haven't even done one deal in their local area yet.

What this means for you as an investor is that if you are doing your first rehab, you should make sure the project does not involve large additions, structural issues, or tear-down houses. If you come from a construction background, then it might be a different story, but if you are new to real estate, then start small or you will pay the price. For example, a townhouse that needs cosmetic work, a condo, or a small house that does not have significant issues would be a great first project. Try to keep the renovation work under 50K unless you come from a background in construction. One of the biggest mistakes I see investors make is underestimating the repair costs and then getting in over their heads.

This is the same type of advice I would give to a new real estate agent. Don't try to start with selling a 5-million-dollar mansion. Don't turn that deal down either, but try to build up experience with the readily available deals first. Maybe start with rental properties on the wrong side of town and get a few of those deals under your belt, build up some experience, and then start doing smaller deals and work your way up to the top. For example, the guys on Million Dollar Listing did not start with those types of houses. Many of them began their career by doing rental properties in bad areas and mastered their craft at each level before moving up.

If you are doing your first wholesale, instead of trying to make a huge profit, focus more on getting the deal done. That is why I always recommend partnering with an experienced and trustworthy wholesaler for your first deal. You can do what's called a co-wholesale, where the top wholesaler in your area can send your wholesale deal out to the thousands of buyers that they have. Working with a top investor increases the likelihood that the deal will go through. If they have a huge buyer's list, which they should, then you can often command a premium price.

As Robert Kiyosaki said, you should try to learn before you earn. If you are doing your first rehab but think it might be too much work, you can also partner with the top local investor in your area. Each investor has a different split, but they will offer options to newer local investors where they provide the funding and construction, and you just have to bring them the deal.

MORAL OF THE STORY: You need to learn

the fundamentals of real estate investing if you want to be successful. That means learning how to generate leads from sellers and evaluating deals. If you are brand new, instead of trying to build a luxury housing development as your first deal, try to find good off-market leads for the top investors in your area first. Then, once you've bird-dogged or wholesaled them a couple of deals, you will get the hang of it and know what to look for in your first potential rehab project. I'm all about evolving to the next level and doing bigger and better deals, but I think you need to start on a smaller scale first.

Making Offers Without Using The MAO Formula

When I was first getting started, my partner and I were buying houses that we thought were good deals, but in reality, they were not even close. Many investors, including myself, assume that if they buy a house at say 200K, put 50K into it, and then sell it at 300K, then they've made a 50K profit. I can't begin to tell you how wrong that way of thinking is and how often I see people assume that.

With real estate investing, especially when you're getting started, you need to use the maximum allowable offer (MAO) formula. This formula gives you a 30% buffer for profit and closing costs, and it is the safest way to buy houses in any market. The MAO formula is an old-school real estate investing principle that goes like this: MAO (maximum allowable offer) equals ARV (after renovated value) times .7 minus the cost of repairs. So if a property sells for 200K renovated and it needs 50K worth of work, then you would take 200K and multiply it by .7 and then subtract 50K to get the price that you could offer. In this scenario, the most you could offer would be 90K.

In some cases, it makes sense to go above that .7 number, if the property will sell for more than 300K or if it does not have a ton of risk, such as a rehab that only needs a little bit of work or is in the best area. The opposite is true as well. If the property is in a bad neighborhood and needs a ton of work, then you might want to go lower than .7, at .65 or even .6.

MORAL OF THE STORY: If you want to save yourself a ton of headaches and money, then I would recommend using this formula for just about any rehab that you take on. Deals that meet the MAO formula take a little bit of time to find, which is good. You need to be very selective when it comes to buying houses.

Overdoing The Renovation For The Area

One of the most common mistakes I see real estate investors make is to overdo a renovation on the house for what the neighborhood is. Before you buy any home, you must do online research of comps so you can get ideas of the popular styles and finishes of the houses that have sold for the highest price in that vicinity. You can make a list of some of these finishes, screenshot what they look like, and even show them to your contractor for what you're looking to get done. I get many of my best renovation ideas from looking at the other houses in the area and cherry-picking the best ideas.

A perfect example of this was a house I looked at in a working-class neighborhood of mostly one-level homes. The investor not only added a massive second story but also put in tens of thousands of dollars of marble throughout the house. The house ended up looking like a weird version of the Taj Mahal, except it was in the suburbs in a working-class community. It did not fit the neighborhood at all and whoever bought the house would most likely have to do another massive renovation just to make the house look somewhat normal. I know this sounds blazingly obvious, but when you are fixing up a property, you need to look at the types of finishes that comparable properties in that neighborhood have done.

You can even steal the best ideas from other houses that have sold and include those in your project. Ask yourself, what type of neighborhood is this? What types of finishes are buyers looking for in this area? Then create your renovation plans around that. The opposite is true as well. If you are in a high-end market, you don't want to use cheap finishes from the sale rack at Home Depot to complete your project.

MORAL OF THE STORY: The moral of this story is that you need to know and understand your comps well. Make sure your level of finishes fit the neighborhood style. You should show your contractors pictures of similar properties that have sold in that neighborhood and what you want your rehab to look like. There is plenty of freely available information online on comparable sales, and you can attend any open houses in your area for good ideas.

Underestimating The Repair Costs

Another common mistake that I have made myself and that almost every new investor makes is not accurately estimating the repairs. I see it happen all the time. Many investors GROSSLY underestimate the cost of repairs when getting started.

Fortunately, there are a couple of ways to make sure this does not happen to you. First of all, you should be networking with other investors at REIAs (Real Estate Investor Associations) and Meetup groups, and listening to what the investors there say it costs to renovate different properties. This will give you a ballpark number to work with. Even some of the house-flipping TV shows out there can give you at least an idea of what different properties cost to renovate. Ideally though, you should itemize in a Google spreadsheet or Excel file all of the potential items that need renovations.

You can also download the repair estimator I like to use for free on my website, www.jeff-leighton.com. Most of the significant expenses you will have to make include replacing the roof, HVAC, kitchen, bathrooms, and windows. Look at HomeAdvisor.com and other similar websites, and start plugging in numbers for what these repairs may cost. The great thing about HomeAdvisor.com and the other repair estimator sites is that they are free and all you have to do is plug in your zip code and the type of repair you will be doing. Then they will give you a low, medium, and high estimate for your repairs. After you have itemized all your repairs and come up with an estimated cost, I would add 10% to whatever number you've come up with. Keep in mind that it is common for contractor estimates to go up and it's not necessarily because the contractor is trying to rip you off or anything.

When doing a project, there are always things you are not expecting that can come up. As a result, the contractor has to change their repair estimate. This is perfectly normal, so you should not be surprised if the repair estimate goes up. It shouldn't go up that drastically, though, which is why we put in 10% instead of 50%. If you have a friend or associate who is a contractor, you can also take them out to lunch or coffee and get an idea of prices and how the business works.

MORAL OF THE STORY: The main idea with repair estimates is to get in the ballpark. Too many investors will be off by a significant amount when it comes to repair estimates. To avoid this, make sure to itemize repairs, talk to other investors on what they are paying for repairs at networking events, and use online resources such as HomeAdvisor.com to get an idea about prices. It wouldn't hurt to take a contractor out to lunch either and ask them about estimates. You should also be using a repair estimator and continuing to educate yourself on the construction side of the business.

SECTION 8

Location, Location, Location

The age-old real estate investment advice of location, location, location is accurate when it comes to flips. Even though a flip is short-term, you need to keep in mind resale value and whether the property you bought could be in a tough area to sell. I am comfortable buying properties in any neighborhood so long as there are renovated comps to support the resale value. However, there are certain things in any area that you need to be aware of.

Some examples of tough locations to sell a house would be on a busy road, in front of a high school, gas station, a condo on the first floor, a home next to a power plan, and other similar obstructions. Even if the house is perfectly renovated, there will be a large percentage of buyers who would not buy any house if it's in those types of locations. That's why, when you run your comps, you need to be sure to run comps that were sold on the same street or in the same vicinity.

A property just a street away could have a drastically different value if it does not have the same obstructions. I once worked with a buyer whom I strongly advised not to buy this one property. It was a property directly in front of a school, on a busy double yellow line road, and in almost tear-down condition. That property would be challenging to re-sell because of all the negative factors. Most likely a builder will purchase that property down the road at a significant discount.

MORAL OF THE STORY: It can be tempting to purchase properties in these less than ideal locations since they are usually a bit lower than the neighborhood comps. I would advise against this because they will take unusually long to sell and you will most likely be selling them at a significant discount compared to comps in the neighborhood. The only time I would say it is okay is if there are sold comps of similar properties along those same, less than ideal locations. If you are the first sold comp, you'd better prepare for a long time on the market and typically for a substantial discount compared to other properties in the neighborhood.

Be Careful Of Partnerships

When getting into real estate investing, it can be very tempting to partner with someone. While some partnerships can be amazing, there are other partnerships that you should avoid at all costs. I always recommend that if you do decide to partner with someone when getting started, you partner with them on a deal-by-deal basis or make sure they have a successful track record of investing. If you do decide to partner with someone, you should be very careful and look out for what we would call "red flags." Several of my real estate partnerships failed in an epic fashion, and every time I should have seen it coming from a thousand miles away. There are three types of people you should avoid working with at all costs.

The first is anyone with a drug problem. While this sounds obvious, you would be surprised how many somewhat successful people have these types of issues. Many people can function and do deals while being high on pills and other drugs. However, the worst thing about working with someone with a drug issue is the people they associate with. I remember days when some of the people my partner wanted to work with would show up with cars that looked like they had just been in a collision, with bruises on their face and wearing court-ordered bracelets around their leg. They would show up to work at any given time of the day and even start asking for money.

Working with these people was a nightmarish circus and to say the least, it was not an ideal working environment. I am not saying this to write off anyone with a drug habit because some amazingly successful people have recovered and done great things in business and life. I am just saying, do not partner with someone who is actively on drugs, no matter how successful they may be or appear to be.

Another type of person to avoid at all costs is

shady people. What I mean by that is if there are recurring instances of dishonesty or anything of that sort, then that should be a red flag. I worked with one person who would do things on a very small scale that I thought was a little strange. It was not until we were in business together that I started to realize the extent of this person's character flaws. If there is any shadiness in someone, it tends to increase to the proportion of the business deal. It does not just go away. That can be a massive problem if you are associated with that person, so try to stay away from that. Confront someone immediately, especially a partner, if there is any type of shadiness or strange behavior.

Lastly, difficult people are probably the most prevalent and annoying people to work with. As you do deals as a real estate investor or agent, there will be two types of people you will work with. There will be other investors, agents, and professionals that are amazing and easy to work with, and then there will be a smaller percentage of people who are super difficult and will make the most menial task a complete headache.

For example, I was in a partnership with

someone who had been sued so much that he decided to go to law school to save money in the future on the inevitable lawsuits he would most likely be a part of. When he told me that, it should have been a red flag. However, somehow I didn't put two and two together. Safe to say, working with this person was a big mistake. However, many times you can nip this issue in the bud by working together on small-scale projects or deals before jumping in head first.

MORAL OF THE STORY: The lessons from this section are to keep an eye out for "red flags," i.e., anything that strikes you as strange, concerning, or out of the normal. There are a couple of ways to prevent these types of partnerships from happening. The first would be to try partnering with someone on a smaller deal or project first, and only on a deal-by-deal basis.

If you can't make it work on a small scale, chances are you can't make it work on a large scale. An initial partnership like that should forecast future collaboration possibilities. You should never have to work with shady people or drug addicts, and this would be the first test. I usually only recommend partnering with the top investors in your area when you are getting started because they have been in the business a while and know how to close deals. Then, once you have experience, you can decide whether partnering with someone else makes sense. Dysfunctional people do not eventually become functional, and trying to change someone is not a good ROI.

The Market Does Not Always Go Up

As a real estate investor doing short-term flips such as rehabs and wholesales, you should never assume that the market will increase. That is exactly how many investors in the 2007 period got into trouble. They would buy houses assuming that the market would keep improving and then they could sell the home without doing any work and make a substantial profit. That is what amateurs do. It's called speculation, not real estate investing.

When you buy houses as a real estate investor, you should take into account the last three sold comparable sales over the previous year. You should not add on 3, 5, or even 10% in appreciation because you think the market will be going up. To be successful in this business, you need to calculate your projects using real numbers, not projected numbers.

The reason hard money lenders can stay in business during up and down markets is precisely that. They use real numbers and only lend at the MAO formula, which means they will lend at 65 or 70% of the after renovated value. That means even if the market were to take a dip, the hard money lender would still be protected because they have built in enough forgiveness with the profit margin.

Only amateurs buy houses on pure speculation. Don't get greedy. Keep in mind the famous quote, "Pigs get fat, hogs get slaughtered." While it is certainly nice if your property goes up during the time that you are renovating and listing it, you should never assume that that will happen and get greedy.

MORAL OF THE STORY: If you want to stay in this business for a long time, then you have to buy houses the way hard money lenders and professional investors do. That means you use the aforementioned MAO formula and you never assume the market will continue to appreciate. It is tough – if not impossible – to predict what the market will do, so only look at previous sales when evaluating deals.

Make Sure You Have The Right Contractor For The Job

When you are doing a property flip, having the right contractors can be the difference between success and failure. I have personally experienced working with the wrong contractors, and it can cause massive delays, headaches, and in some cases even legal issues.

In this part of the book, I will show you how to find the best contractors. You should spend most of your time pre-screening contractors when getting into a rehab. That will save you time on the backend since chances are you won't have to fire them or hire additional contractors.

For starters, you should have more than one contractor available and compile a database of contractors that you can reference at any given time. There are a couple of quick ways to build up a solid list of quality, vetted contractors. The first is from referrals from any real estate investing groups, investors, or agents. Also, ask anyone you know that recently had work done on their house for recommendations for contractors.

The second way to find contractors is that anytime you are driving around neighborhoods where you would potentially be doing a flip, you should look for houses that have work being done on them. Many times, the contractor will have their sign in the front yard with contact information. If not, you can just park your car and ask them for a card. Let them know you might be doing renovations soon and you are looking for good contractors. You typically only want to hire contractors that are busy, which goes for hiring anyone. Usually, if they are working, it's because they are good and will get the job done.

Lastly, I would recommend visiting local real estate agents' websites and clicking on the part of their site that says "preferred vendors." Most of the top real estate agents will have a list of the contractors they recommend, and you can add more contractors to your list that way. Once you have created a list of contractors using these three strategies, I suggest to cross-reference them with online reviews and make sure they have a license and insurance.

Out of the list that you now have, you should be able to find several that come recommended or are actively working, have good online reviews, AND are properly licensed and insured. If you can find contractors that check all three boxes, then the likelihood of them doing an excellent job for you is significantly higher than some contractor you might find randomly find on Craigslist or at Home Depot.

MORAL OF THE STORY: Contractors are the key between a successful flip and a non-successful flip, so be sure to spend a lot of time screening and searching for the best ones. I can tell you first-hand that the time you spend up front doing research will save you time and money on the backend. Start building your database today. With the aforementioned strategies, you should easily have at least 10-15 contractors on your list.

Avoid This When Listing Your Property

I've seen a lot of first-time real estate investors try to save money on their rehabs by listing the property themselves as an FSBO, or for sale by owner. Since most sellers have to pay a real estate commission of 6% (3% to buyer's agent and 3% to listing agent), they think they will save that money by doing it themselves.

Here's the truth on FSBOs. I have seen hundreds of these types of deals. Everybody thinks they can list a property and become an agent. Anyone can get their license and become a real estate agent, but in reality very few people become successful full-time agents out of all the people that get licensed. Just because you have your license does not mean you will do a good job.

Additionally, most agents do not like to show for-sale-by-owner properties because they are typically not listed on the MLS and these sellers have a reputation of being completely unrealistic and difficult to work with. Many FSBOs will just list their property to see if they can reach for a high price, so they already have a reputation of being priced too high. These types of properties feel "janky" since the listing is done by an amateur. If you don't know what "janky" means, the definition according to the *Oxford Dictionary* is "of extremely poor or unreliable quality." Any potential buyer of this property will think to themselves that if the seller is trying to cut the corner on real estate commissions, then what else are they cutting corners on when it comes to their property?

Instead, as a seller, you need to do three things to ensure your property sells quickly and at the right price. The first is to find a local, highly recommended real estate agent. You can do that by looking at for sale signs in the neighborhood, asking referrals from friends and family that have sold recently, and doing online research. A good local agent will know exactly what to list it for, have experience with that type of property, and maybe even have buyers in their database for it.

The next thing you need to do is have professional photography done on your property. Now, a good agent will include a professional photographer taking pictures of your property. Be sure not to skimp on this. Many people will eliminate a house just from the photos. I can't tell you how many times I've shown a buyer a house they were not very high on because the pictures were so bad, but when we showed up, the house was terrific. If you don't think photographs are that big of a deal, you should read about how Airbnb became so popular. The biggest reason they became such a huge business was that they get professional photos done instead of dark images on a cell phone camera. Airbnb hires professional photographers for free if you have a listing with them because they understand how important the photos are. Always get these done.

Lastly, the third thing you need to do to get your property sold fast and for a high price is staging. I admit that when I was getting started, I thought it was a little bit of a gimmick. However, I can assure you that it is not a gimmick and it will help get your property sold fast. Most real estate agents should include this in their listing. Vacant houses without staging feel cold, smaller, and sterile. Staging can help you envision what it's like to live in the property. Most of the top investors I know get their properties staged.

MORAL OF THE STORY: I can't emphasize enough that you should not do an FSBO. The bottom line is, you need to use a highly recommended full-time local real estate agent, get professional photos, and have the property staged professionally. This does not mean you take the pictures yourself or that you try to stage the property yourself. I have seen many failed attempts of agents trying to be professional photographers or trying to stage a property. There are professionals who offer these services for a reasonable fee. Having professional photos, staging, and using a recommended real estate agent will get your property sold FAST and for the highest amount. Also, don't worry about finding a professional photographer or stager; your agent will have both of those. If they don't, then find another agent.

SECTION 13

⸎————⸎

Run Your Own Numbers

Once you start networking and getting involved in the real estate investing community, you will begin to receive deals via email, text, or even phone calls. Wholesalers and real estate agents who know that you buy houses will send you potential fixer-upper properties that could be good deals.

There is one thing you should make sure to do with all of these deals: run your own numbers. Just because a wholesaler or an agent sends you over a deal and says that you could sell it for 500K renovated does not make it true. You need to run that deal through your own deal analysis independently. I get deals all the time from wholesalers who say a property could sell for X amount, but they might be using old comps or sales from a different neighborhood. I treat a lead from a wholesaler or real estate agent the same way I would with any lead; I run all my numbers and then decide whether or not it's a deal. 90% of the leads I generate or am referred to, I do not pursue because they are so far off on price.

I'm not saying the wholesaler or real estate agent is trying to trick you, but you need to be realistic and conservative with your numbers. If you are new to real estate investing and you think you may have a deal but you're not sure, one thing you can do is run it by a local hard money lender or another local investor that you know and trust. They can usually tell you within minutes whether or not it's a good deal. You should use the MAO formula for all of your deals. If it's at the MAO formula or close to it, then it could be a great deal. However, a good rule of thumb is, if it's far off from the MAO formula, then chances are it's not a good deal.

MORAL OF THE STORY: While you should try to recruit and network with as many wholesalers and real estate agents as possible to find deals, you should also perform your own analysis of any deal. The best investors in any area might get 20 or even 50 leads a month from wholesalers and agents. At the end of the month though, they might only end up buying one or two of those deals. Make sure to use the MAO formula and verify the comps that any wholesaler or agent is sending you.

SECTION 14

Trusting Everyone

In real estate investing and any other business, there are mostly good companies with good reputations. I honestly do not see this business as a cut-throat type of business where everyone is out for themselves. In fact, I am good friends with many of my direct competitors. I see them all as potential partners and not even as competition. However, there will occasionally be rotten apples you need to watch out for. I once had a shady company steal a deal from me, and I have no one to blame but myself.

You need to get offers in writing with real estate. Sometimes sellers may verbally agree to a price but not actually sign anything. Especially if you are wholesaling a deal, you need to make sure you have the contract signed before you present the deal to your end buyer. I once showed a great deal opportunity to a local house buyer whom I didn't really know. All I knew about them was that they had bought a similar house in that neighborhood, which usually is a good sign. A couple of days later, after sending them the deal, I found out they had gone behind my back and signed directly with the seller. Now, we did pursue legal options in terms of getting the deal back, but all of this could have been prevented if I had done a couple of things differently.

Number one, you need to get everything in writing. In most cases, you should try to get any deal signed before presenting it to another investor. Secondly, if you are going to show a deal to another investor without getting the property under contract first, make sure they are legitimate. Sometimes you may get a lead that you are not sure about. You think it's a good deal, but you don't want to risk putting it under contract. In that scenario, it is okay to send that lead to a top local buyer in your area to see what they think about it, but I would not blast it out on your buyer's list.

Keep in mind it is not the top buyers that typically screw you over. It's the smaller operators who may not do that many deals. If I had properly researched this company, I would have found bad online reviews, different legal issues they were dealing with, and in general, not many people that could vouch for them. I looked them up recently and they are not even in business anymore, which was gratifying. Always be aware of whom you are selling to.

MORAL OF THE STORY: The moral of the story is that you should get offers in writing. If you are not sure about a deal, then only send it out to someone you know, like, and trust. I also don't want you to be paranoid, thinking that everyone is out to steal your deal because only a small percentage of people will do this type of thing. The overwhelming majority of investors are honest and easy to work with. When in doubt, work with the top home buyers.

—◆—————◆—————◆—

Quitting Your Full-Time Job Too Soon

Real estate investing can be very exciting, especially if your current job has you doing the same thing day in and day out. Most aspiring real estate investors dream about quitting their desk job and living the life as a real estate entrepreneur. It can be tempting to quit your job the moment you find your first big deal; however, I would like to throw in some words of caution.

Cash flow is king in the business world. I would only recommend quitting your job to become a full-time real estate investor after you have completed at least three successful deals. I know too many real estate investors who start counting the profit they will make the minute they get a property under contract.

In reality, it can take up to six months before you see a profit on some rehabs. When wholesaling a deal, you can flip the deal within 30 days. However, I would always recommend waiting until the deal closes and until you have three deals under your belt before you quit your job. You need to learn how to build consistency in this business because when you are starting out, you won't get consistent bi-monthly paychecks as you do at a job. Real estate investing money comes in chunks, so some months you might not get paid at all while other months you may make the entire yearly salary that you made at your previous job.

MORAL OF THE STORY: Don't quit your day job just yet. Close at least three deals so that you can get the hang of the business and still have the luxury of consistent paychecks from your job. You can even keep your full-time job if you are building up a rental portfolio so that you have the income to buy more and more rentals. Then, once the cash flow reaches a certain amount, you can quit.

I see way too many investors who find their first deal, immediately quit their job, and then end up in a cash flow crunch. In addition, once you officially quit your job, you could pick up a part-time job with another local agent or investor to keep the steady cash flow coming in, gain more experience, and hang out with people since the life of a start-up real estate entrepreneur can be lonely at times.

Falling In Love With A House Instead Of The Numbers

I see this issue happen with newer investors all the time. It has happened to me too. An investor will come across a property, and maybe it's an ideal location or the house has an interesting style that could look amazing once it's fixed up. Either way, the investor falls into the trap of falling in love with the house instead of falling in love with the numbers.

Even though you may think the house is fantastic, it still needs to come down to numbers. If the numbers don't work, I don't care if it's the perfect house for me in the ideal neighborhood; I still won't buy it. Not only that, but I would prefer to buy the ugliest house in the most crime-ridden neighborhood if the numbers look better.

People ask me all the time what neighborhood I prefer to buy homes in. My answer is, whatever area has the best numbers on the deal. That could be in the best neighborhood or the worst neighborhood, although I typically try to stay within a 30-minute radius around my city. Think about it like this. There is a good price for any property. If there is a tear-down house in front of a gas station on a busy road and all the other tear-downs in front of gas stations sell for 100K, then 50K could be a great deal, even if the house and location are terrible.

MORAL OF THE STORY: Fall in love with numbers, not houses. I have seen amazing mid-century modern homes that I would love to buy and fix up, and they would look spectacular. However, the numbers don't always work. In fact, you could lose a lot of money on a deal like that. Fall in love instead with running accurate numbers, finding solid comps in the area, and coming up with a solid repair estimate. That is how you will be successful in this business.

Not Screening Your Tenants

When I bought my first rental investment property, I was thrilled. Here I was with my own piece of real estate, and I had visions of purchasing 10 or 20 more of these rentals over the next couple of years. With all the excitement of buying my first property, I forgot one essential part of being a successful landlord.

I put the ad for a renter out online and got many responses. The property was in good condition and reasonably inexpensive for the area. One of the potential applicants I got told me she was willing to pay $100 more per month to rent and that the county paid half of her rent, so it would be easy for her to make payments. I was excited! Not only had I already found a potential renter, but they were willing to pay $100 more than anybody else. I immediately agreed to rent out the property to her without doing any credit or background check of any type. While I did have a lease agreement, I did not do the proper due diligence that any good real estate investor or property management company would typically do.

The first month was great: I got my rental check and I was making my first passive income. However, within about two months, things started to go downhill fast. I got a message from the tenant saying that she could pay half of the rent, but the other half would be a little late. I was a little annoyed, but I told her to get it to me when she could.

Another month went by with only half the payment and another, and soon I realized that she did not have any money to pay the rent. I was coming out of pocket to pay for a place someone else was living in, and I was not thrilled. I asked her what was going on and tried to work something out, but things were going downhill fast, and I was hemorrhaging money at an alarming rate from this property every month.

The only option was to evict the tenant as soon as possible if I were to keep the property above water and not get foreclosed on. I studied up on my landlord laws of the state and the next day I filed the eviction proceedings. Fortunately for me, the state I owned the property in is very landlord-friendly. If a tenant is not paying rent, you can usually evict within about 30 days. The sheriff posted a note on her door the next day and the proceedings started.

Fortunately, I did not have to hire a lawyer since the paperwork was fairly straightforward. Within a couple of weeks, the tenant was gone and had left my place a trash pit. Not only that, but she had painted the entire unit pink. Since this was just a small condo, I got a cleaning and painting crew in there the next day and they were able to make it shine again.

MORAL OF THE STORY: When you are first getting started in real estate investing, it is very exciting and it can be tempting to think that everyone will do what he or she say they will do.

However, there is a reason that you screen tenants or even potential business partners. If you are going to own rentals properties, I would recommend paying a property management company to screen tenants for you. Ask them what type of screening they do and how much experience they have. It should be in the property management company's best interest to find a long-term, financially stable, low-maintenance tenant. If you decide to lease the property yourself, make sure to do a credit check, background check, and verify employment or see bank statements before you rent to anybody.

---◆◆◆---

Getting To The Next Level As A Real Estate Investor

One of the biggest mistakes I see real estate investors make is not having an open mindset about learning new skills and strategies. The vast majority of real estate professionals are missing out on insider information by not seeking further knowledge through books, seminars, mentors, and mastermind events. If you want to get to the next level as a real estate investor and then the next level after that, you need to find people at the top of the business and get information directly from them. In this next section, I will give you two examples of people that I have met in my real estate career. I have changed their names for obvious reasons.

Meet Bill. Bill is an old-school type of guy who has been in the real estate investing business for 20 years now. He is somewhat successful in his own right. He likes to get his hands dirty on each of the projects that he does and tries to do all the work himself. Bill doesn't believe in attending seminars or reading books on real estate investing because in his words "there's nothing you can learn in a book that you can't learn out in the real world."

As a result, Bill's business has looked the same over the last couple of decades and probably will look the same in the next 10 or 20 years. Bill doesn't know what he doesn't know, and even though he probably has more experience than 90 percent of real estate investors out there, he is missing out on information that could help him do more deals and work less by creating systems and outsourcing parts of his business.

Meet Tyler. Tyler is a hungry, motivated real estate investor who has immersed himself in books, seminars, and even sought out mentors in the real estate investing world who are 5, 10, or even 20 years ahead of him. By seeking out these mentors who are so far ahead of him, he can see into the future and decide what kind of business he wants to create for himself. The books he reads and seminars he attends teach him new exit strategies with real estate investing, such as wholesaling, as well as new marketing tactics that allow him to get over 100 leads per month.

Even though Tyler just got started in the business, he now has rehab projects going on, wholesales, and he is even building up his resources to lend money to other local investors at a 12% yearly rate. He is also mentoring other local up-and-coming investors and splits deals with them 50/50 in exchange for the mentorship. Because Tyler has exposed himself to so many new ideas and has constantly been learning and applying new concepts from all the teachings, he has now already passed Bill. He is doing more deals in less time and has left poor Bill in the dust.

MORAL OF THE STORY: Don't be a one-trick pony. Too many of the old-school investors are missing out on tremendous opportunities because they can't get their blinders off. All of the

The Real Estate Investor Survival Guide

top investors I know are continually learning and even attending some of the seminars they have gone to the past three, four, or even five times so that they can internalize the information and learn new things every year. As the real estate investing market is constantly changing, you need to associate yourself with the best training and latest books so that you can maximize your business to earn more and work less. I like to think of myself as version 1.0, 2.0, 3.0. Each year I'm getting better at investing, learning new strategies, becoming more powerful, and taking my game to the next level.

~ 70 ~

No Leads = No Deals

If you want to be a full-time investor in the real estate business, you need to have a marketing machine. You should try to do what Jay Abraham says and build a marketing Parthenon. Instead of relying on just one source of leads, you need to develop multiple pillars or, in other words, multiple sources of leads and deals. This could be networking, direct mail, online marketing, and any other strategies you implement.

When I was getting started as an investor, what I would do is put a lot of resources towards marketing and getting leads. Then, as soon as I got a property, I would stop all marketing and focus on getting the deal rehabbed and sold. As a result of stopping all marketing efforts, my leads dried up, and I would get no deals until that property was sold and I could do more lead generation. You need to think of marketing as the lifeblood of your business. No leads equal no deals.

Now I have systems in place where, when I get a property under contract, I still do marketing every single week to find the next deal. If you are a newer investor, I would always recommend doing a wholesale as your first deal because it allows you to get cash in your pocket fast so that you can send out more marketing and find more deals. Moreover, if you are not sure about how to structure a wholesale, just reach out to the top local investors in your area, the people you see buying houses and advertising everywhere and let them know you have a potential deal to wholesale. They often have joint venture programs where they can send your deal out on their list, and then you split the profit. If you decide to do a rehab, then make sure to leverage other people's money so that you still have resources to put towards marketing. You don't want to have all your money tied up in a rehab with no funds for marketing.

MORAL OF THE STORY: You need to always be marketing in this business. The great thing about real estate investing is that lead generation is predictable. I know if I send out X amount of postcards or letters, I will most likely get a one- or two-percent response rate. Or, if I talk to 10 wholesalers, I will probably get at least one qualified lead per week. If you are not doing marketing or networking, you will not get any deals. Keep that in mind when you decide to take on a wholesale or rehab. I would recommend doing your marketing once per week, rain or shine. That is how you will gain consistency in this business and go from doing one deal per year to one deal per month.

SECTION 20

Burning Bridges

The real estate investment business is a small circle of people, no matter how large your city is, and word spreads quick. There are many investors I know that don't seem to keep this in mind. If you screw someone over trying to make a quick buck or if you are a pain in the ass to deal with, your reputation will be known soon.

Whether it's at networking events such as REIAs, Meetups, or just talking real estate with other fellow investors, you will find out quickly who to stay away from. Have you ever been to a real estate happy hour before? Every time I go, I feel like it should be called the real estate gossip hour.

I just sit back and hear all these stories about who

is good to work with and who you should avoid at all costs. No matter what you do, you should keep in mind your reputation and try not to burn any bridges. The reason is that you will probably see this person or company again in the near future. If you back out of a wholesale deal or don't close on a deal that you had under contract, chances are no one will want to send you deals anymore.

For example, take one investor I know who is known as being a difficult person who is hard to work with. He takes pride in this. As a result, his reputation suffers, and the number of real estate professionals who want to work with him is extremely limited. He mostly works with people who are new to the business and don't know any better.

MORAL OF THE STORY: You need to protect your reputation as a stand-up business type of person. Keep in mind that if you screw someone over or people have a negative experience working with you, then there will be a ripple effect. This is a small community. It's like a small town in Texas; everybody knows everybody, people talk about different deals that went through and fell apart. If you burn bridges with someone, be prepared to run into that person in the future.

Focus On Getting To Closing

When you are new to real estate investing, it is very exciting. When you get your first deal under contract, it can be easy to think that you will make an enormous profit. You will typically see one comp in the neighborhood that sold for a significantly higher price than the comps, and you will think that you can sell your deal for the same price even though the majority of the comps are much lower. This is wrong. You need to be more conservative with your first couple of deals. You should focus more on getting the deal done and building experience than trying to make a massive profit. Let me tell you a story about one of my first deals.

I locked up a property in an up-and-coming part of the city, the perfect deal for investors. Excitedly, I marked up the price of my wholesale deal because I saw that a property on that street had sold for the same price. Of course, I didn't even keep in mind that that property was more upgraded than the fixer-upper I was selling. When I went to email out my wholesale deal, absolutely no one was interested in it at that price. I didn't even get a reply.

That can be pretty scary if it's your first wholesale deal and you can't even find a buyer. What I did to get the deal sold was co-wholesale it with another local investor who knew the prices better and who had a larger buyers list. We were able to make a big profit off of this strategy, but I learned not to get too greedy with the price.

MORAL OF THE STORY: When you are getting started with real estate investing, it can be very tempting to get greedy on your first wholesale or rehab deal since you don't know any better. That is why I always recommend partnering with another, more experienced wholesaler for your first deal. If you are doing a rehab, start with a smaller project and make sure you use the MAO formula when evaluating the property. Just because one comp in the neighborhood sold for a high price does not mean yours will sell for that same price. You need to have at least two or, better yet, three comparable sales to use if you want to sell it for that higher price. I see newer wholesalers do this all the time. I might get an email from them saying that the after renovated property is much higher than what the actual value might be. I can often tell it might be their first deal. Focus more on just getting several successful deals under your belt before you try to make a significant profit on any deal.

Become Friends
With The Seller

When you get a motivated seller lead and you plan on making an offer, you need to build as much rapport with the seller as possible. There are a couple of reasons for this. Try to talk to the seller like a friend instead of like a corporation where someone is calling a 1-800 number and acting stifled.

To begin with, nobody likes talking to someone who clearly only cares about business. You should ask questions about the property and not talk about how bad it is. Too many investors I know will completely trash the property in front of the seller. I have gotten deals where I offered less, but the seller just liked me more. The second reason for building rapport is that if something goes wrong with the deal, which can sometimes happen, you need to have some forgiveness built in.

I was working with one seller and had been professional, established rapport, and was responsive to them the whole time. About a week after getting the property under contract, I realized that the front foundation of the house would need to be repaired, which is not an easy fix. I called her back, told her about the issue with the property, and explained we would need to be about 15K lower than our initial offer price.

If this were someone that I had not built up a rapport with, they probably would go to the next buyer since they had received numerous letters. I was able to save the deal, though, because I was responsive, professional, honest and had built up a rapport. The seller agreed to drop the price of the house by 15K and we were able to get the deal done.

MORAL OF THE STORY: Always try to build up as much positive rapport as possible with the seller because with real estate investing there can be delays and things that come up. It is called the bank of goodwill, and you need to build as much goodwill as possible in the beginning and throughout the deal. Sometimes you might need to close a week later than expected, or you might come across an unexpected repair item. You want to have enough goodwill built in with the seller so that, if something comes up, it does not derail the deal.

—◆—

Every Neighborhood Is Great

When investors are getting started, a lot of them will try to focus on just one neighborhood. While starting locally is always a great idea, you should increase your parameters to a radius of 30 minutes or so around where you live, instead of focusing one small pocket of a neighborhood that you want to buy houses in.

I live in an urban area. There are about seven different large counties and cities all within about 30 minutes from me. I got started thinking that I would just focus on my own neighborhood. The first marketing I did was sending out mailers and doing some online ads. While this initial strategy was generating me leads every single month, it was not until I replicated that same strategy in all seven counties that I started to see lots of deals and tons of leads.

Of course, I would prefer to do deals a block or two away from where I live. However, sometimes the most lucrative deal might be 15 or 20 minutes away, in a neighborhood that is not my first choice. Having been a real estate investor for many years now, I have come to realize that I don't care where the property is. I care more about the deal itself. The best deal might be in the worst neighborhood and vice versa. It should all come down to numbers and comparable sales in that area. As long as I'm not driving more than 45 minutes or so to get to the house, then I am okay with doing the deal.

MORAL OF THE STORY: Try to expand your real estate investing area. I don't mean trying to buy houses three states away, even though there are some real estate investors who start doing deals in their own market and then expand nationally. If you want to do more deals, you should increase the radius around where you market to motivated sellers.

Instead of marketing to motivated sellers in just one county, I now do the same marketing in seven counties, and I never run out of leads or deals. With real estate flipping, you are not buying houses for future appreciation and you are not buying homes to live in. You should not be falling in love with a house or an area. Instead, you need to fall in love with the numbers on the deal, which could come from any neighborhood.

SECTION 24

Protect Your Assets

Every now and then, as a real estate investor, you might be purchasing properties in not so great neighborhoods. As a battle-hardened real estate investor, I can tell you that sometimes in these areas you might have your appliances stolen, your copper pipes ripped out, or the house might be vandalized. Fortunately, there is a simple way to solve this issue.

Security systems these days have become more and more affordable and much more user-friendly. If you ever go to an electronics depot type of store, you will find many security systems of all sorts, some which are very cool and innovative. I recently went to one electronics store and spent over an hour just checking out all the cool security methods for a property. Since this is only an investment property and not your personal residence, I would recommend going with something that is quick, inexpensive, and reliable.

Although the systems are always changing, the best one I have found is called SimpliSafe. As the name says, it is simple and keeps your property safe. The set comes with about four or five different pieces that you stick on to any doors, window, or potential access points. Then you also have a keypad for your security code and a motion sensor that you can place in the kitchen, living room, or entrance area.

For a couple of hundred bucks, you can get your house set up and then for an additional small fee per month, SimpliSafe will monitor the home for you and alert you to any activity. At the last property I bought I had to set up a system ASAP since my appliances had just been stolen and I had a feeling the copper pipes were probably next. I set up the system in about 15 minutes, tested it out, and found it very user-friendly. Another security measure I would take is put a metal cage around your AC unit. Any contractor can install that for you, and any local Home Depot or Lowes typically has cages.

MORAL OF THE STORY: As an investor, you will purchase properties in high-end and low-end areas. I have bought houses in some neighborhoods where I had no problem leaving the door unlocked, while other neighborhoods I would be hesitant to drive there at night. To ensure that your house is not vandalized or does not get appliances or pipes stolen, I would recommend a security system. As far as I can tell, SimpliSafe is the best one on the market for a quick, effective, and affordable way to protect your home.

SECTION 25

Becoming Known In The Community

As a real estate investor, you should network as much as humanly possible. Not only will you meet possible joint venture partners, investors, private money lenders, contractors, and more, but you will also learn a lot from attending local REIAs, Meetup groups, and any other type of real estate networking. Do not try to be too cool for school and think you are above going to these events. While many of the people at REIAs and in Meetup groups are beginner real estate investors, I can guarantee you some people there are ten levels above you.

In any given city there will be at least one REIA

or real estate investor association. In some cases, there are several REIAs, all of which might have different styles. There are four in my general vicinity. Some of them are run professionally and some are not, but either way I can tell you, you will always learn something at a REIA. Even at the worst-run REIA, there will be at least one or two full-time real estate investors that are completely crushing it. The best thing about going to REIAs is that it is an easy-to-implement networking strategy that anyone can do.

There are also local Meetup real estate investing groups that are similar to REIAs, which you can find on Meetup.com. These are also great to attend because you will learn the topic of the day and have ample time to network with the local investment community. They will go over case studies of recent deals in their neighborhood as well as what they are paying to renovate properties and other valuable information. Keep in mind that the best investors always have the most extensive network, so try to build yours as much as possible.

MORAL OF THE STORY: Real estate investing comes down to marketing and networking. You should never think that you are above networking, and it's amazing how many high-level people you will meet at a REIA. Most people think there might only be one REIA in their local area, but if you live near a big city, chances are there are several REIAs and several separate Meetup groups for real estate investors. You should put all of them on your calendar and try to immerse yourself in the community. These events will help you build your real estate team and allow you to learn a lot. The more people you know, the more deals you will do.

Conclusion

———◆———

In the end, mistakes make you a better real estate investor. However, I hope you can learn from the mistakes that and my investor friends and I have made. You can save a ton of money and headaches by carefully reviewing the moral of each story and making sure you don't do the same thing. While it is impossible to avoid all mistakes, this overview should give you an advantage over the competition.

Also, don't let the fear of making a mistake paralyze you from taking action. I have found that as long as I take action with my marketing and I do the right thing in business, deals usually work out. What I love about real estate is that every single deal you do, whether you make 1K or 100K profit, you learn a ton about the business, and it makes you savvier and more experienced for the next deal.

I noticed a huge difference in myself as an

investor from doing my first deal, to my first five deals, to my first 20 deals, and on and on. You expand as an investor by doing deals and seeking out knowledge like what you find in this book. If you want to be successful, I recommend starting small in your backyard and getting a real estate mentor.

About The Author

Jeff Leighton is a real estate investor, real estate broker, and bestselling Amazon Author. He has been mentored by some of the top real estate investors in the US and continues to invest in real estate to this day. Over the last several years, he has taught thousands of people around the world on how to get started in real estate investing.

Want More Training?

Go to www.jeff-leighton.com for helpful videos, free resources, downloads, additional mentoring, online programs, and much, much more. You can also text **DEAL to 345345** to stay updated on everything we have going on in the real estate investing world.

Other Books By The Author

Available on Amazon

Follow Jeff Leighton

Instagram.com/J_Late12
YouTube.com/JeffLeighton1
Facebook.com/JeffLeighton5